MW00961786

The New York Co-op Apartment Buyer's Guide

Real-Life Insights on Renting versus Buying, Mortgages, Tax Benefits, Ownership Costs, and the Complete Purchase Process

Reader Advisory:

This book is not intended to serve as professional financial or legal advice. The information provided is based solely on my personal experiences and views during my own co-op apartment purchasing process. While I aim to offer helpful insights and practical tips, please consult with a professional advisor or financial expert before making any decisions regarding your real estate investments or purchases.

Contents

Acknowledgements

I would like to express my heartfelt gratitude to my close friends Adrian Tsou and Luis Alamilla for their invaluable support and guidance throughout the writing process of this book. Their deep understanding of me at a personal level has influenced how I present myself in relation to this book. As reviewers and advisors, their insights and opinions have helped me uncover unique aspects of my experiences that I may not have discovered on my own. Adrian, a talented digital architect, artist, and DJ from Los Angeles, has provided me with valuable feedback and unwavering support in completing this book. Luis, an esteemed video game reviewer who also works at 505 Games in Los Angeles, has contributed his exceptional writing skills and expertise in effectively conveying key points. I am particularly grateful to Luis for writing a personal reference letter for my co-op application, which demonstrates his deep understanding of my personality.

I would like to extend my gratitude to Clarissa Tong, a dear friend and talented illustrator from San Diego. Clarissa has been one of my closest friends since my first visit to the United States for an English learning program at the University of California, San Diego, where she was my first conversation partner. We exchanged English and Japanese languages, and her engaging and humorous drawings perfectly capture the warmth and bright side of people and things. From the beginning, I knew I wanted her artistic touch in this book, and her illustrations have added an extra layer of creativity and charm. As a former English teacher in Toyama, Japan, Clarissa not only knows me well but also possesses a keen eye for visual storytelling.

Furthermore, I want to express my sincere appreciation to Yukihiro Mitsuno, one of my closest friends in NYC. Yukihiro and I have had numerous discussions, from assessing co-op purchases to various personal financial topics, including the ramifications of continuing to rent. His experience in the co-op purchasing process, combined with his knowledge of personal financial decision-making and his familiarity with the NYC market and its historical trends, have been invaluable. I am grateful for his guidance, and I deeply appreciate his presence during the second viewing of the co-op, a crucial moment that helped solidify my decision. Additionally, his personal reference letter for the co-op board further exemplified his understanding of my journey.

Lastly, I would like to express my deepest appreciation to my representative broker and attorney, whose professionalism and clear communication have been essential in guiding me through the nerve-wracking process of purchasing my first co-op. Their responsiveness, patience in addressing my questions, and commitment to providing trustworthy and reliable guidance have been paramount to my success. I am thankful for their expertise and for ensuring that this experience was both seamless and fulfilling.

To Adrian, Luis, Clarissa, Yukihiro, my representative broker, and my attorney, thank you for your unwavering support, invaluable contributions, and dedication. This book and my co-op purchase journey would not have been possible without each one of you. Your expertise, insights, and friendship have played a vital role, and I am forever grateful for our collaboration and shared experiences. Your contributions not only enriched this

Acknowledgements

book but also made the co-op purchase journey a fulfilling and memorable experience.

I would also like to express my gratitude to all those who have supported me throughout this writing process and co-op purchase journey. Your encouragement, guidance, and friendship have been instrumental in bringing this book to fruition and making this milestone a reality. Thank you for being by my side.

CHAPTER 1

Introduction

Welcome! I am delighted to have you here. Allow me to introduce myself. I'm Kento, the author of this guide that will accompany you through the intricate world of cooperative (co-op) building purchases. Whether you are a seasoned New Yorker or a fresh face in the city, this book is tailor-made to equip you with the knowledge and insights needed to make informed decisions from start to finish. This guide aims to provide a comprehensive overview of the co-op purchasing process and empower you to make well-informed decisions.

Let me start by sharing why I wrote this book and what you can expect to discover within its pages: a few years ago, I developed a keen interest in real estate, particularly in co-op buildings. In early 2021, I embarked on a journey of educating myself about co-op purchases, despite having no prior experience in real estate transactions. I delved into extensive reading, watched countless YouTube videos, and engaged in conversations with co-op owners and real estate brokers. Through these experiences, I gained valuable insights that shaped my thought process and approach to my co-op purchasing journey. In this book, I have made it my mission to guide you through the labyrinth of co-op purchases, offering practical insights and valuable information every step of the way. From understanding market dynamics and financial considerations to maneuvering the board approval process and conducting thorough due diligence, I'll elaborate on every step. By sharing my knowledge and experiences, I aim to empower you to make well-informed decisions and discover the perfect co-op to suit your needs and aspirations.

New York City is a melting pot of cultures and communities, and its thriving Japanese community blends seamlessly with the diverse mix of US and international cultures. People in New York are open to new ideas, and the city offers the convenience of not relying on a car to get around. Instead, you can easily navigate the city by using public transportation or walking. No more issues dealing with Google Maps, angry drivers, parking woes, or car-related stress. As for the weather, winters in New York are not as intense as I thought, and with a warm jacket, you will be perfectly comfortable. Summers can be tough, but they make people appreciate the spring and fall seasons even more, despite their brevity. The unique rhythm of the city is something you will not find anywhere else.

Having experienced life in Kyoto, Japan, as well as cities like San Diego and Los Angeles, I have come to appreciate the unique charm and complexities of New York. Its vibrant energy, diverse neighborhoods, and rich cultural offerings make it an unparalleled place to call home. However, along with its tremendous benefits, New York also presents unique challenges, particularly in the realm of housing. As rent prices continue to soar and the cost of living becomes increasingly burdensome, purchasing a co-op offers an opportunity to establish roots and find stability in this ever-changing city.

Whether you are a first-time buyer or a seasoned investor, this book will serve as your trusted compass, helping you navigate the complexities of the New York City's real estate market. So, whether you find yourself captivated by the dazzling lights of Times Square, enchanted by the peaceful streets of the West Village, or utterly mesmerized by the cultural melting pot of Queens, consider this book your unwavering guide. Together, let us embark on this exhilarating journey and unlock the door to your dream co-op in the vibrant city of New York.

Introduction of the author:

Let me introduce myself and share some insights into my personal financial situation and lifestyle, so you can understand how it relates to your own. Thoroughly understanding your personal situation is fundamental to your decision-making process when it comes to purchasing an apartment and selecting your living situation. You can replace my information with your personal story as you read the rest of the chapter. As you are more familiar with your desires and other factors that influence your decision-making, you can align your choices with your specific needs and aspirations.

As a manager in an accounting firm, my W-2 income falls within the typical industry average salary range of $130,000 to $170,000, including discretionary bonuses during prosperous years. I am currently employed under an H1B work authorization visa, which grants me the ability to work in the United States. As an H1B visa holder, I am aware of the unique challenges and considerations that come with this immigration status. The H1B visa is initially valid for three years and can be renewed for another three years, totaling a maximum of six years. Typically, during this period, the visa sponsor employer will initiate the process of sponsoring a permanent visa. I am currently in the process of obtaining a permanent visa, which provides stability and long-term opportunities in the United States.

Introduction

I have lived in various neighborhoods throughout my time in the U.S., including Williamsburg, Elmhurst, and Upper West Side. Currently, I reside in the Upper East Side of Manhattan with a spacious studio apartment at an excellent monthly rent of $2,000, given the current market conditions that would be averaged around $2,500 (Renthop, 2024). In terms of my lifestyle, I enjoy playing soccer and golf during my free time and cherish moments spent with friends. I live a modest lifestyle, cooking meals at home, indulging in reading, and taking one or two vacations each year to explore new destinations. I visit my parents in Japan annually. These details about my own circumstances and choices shape my journey and influence the decisions I have made regarding cooperative ownership after careful assessment. Life choices never guarantee 100% of the desired outcome, and if you wait for the percentage to increase, you might miss the timing, as circumstances can change negatively. I usually go for a decision with 75% conviction, acknowledging that there is always 25% risk due to various uncertainties.

As we navigate the cooperative purchase process together, I believe you will find valuable insights and guidance applicable to your own unique situation. As a New Yorker, I am mindful of my personal finance while embracing the vibrant lifestyle the city offers. The decision to invest in a primary residential apartment aligns with my commitment to financial responsibility and long-term stability. During the COVID-19 pandemic, my work transitioned to a completely remote setting, promoting me to test living in Los Angeles. While the experience was enlightening, I found that the energy, infrastructure, and diverse community of New York City resonated with me in a way that Los Angeles did not. This realization played a pivotal role in reaffirming my decision to pursue cooperative ownership, highlighting the unique qualities of New York City that make it feel like home.

Growing up in Kyoto, my hometown in Japan, I find similarities between the lifestyle in New York City and the experiences I had in Kyoto. Both cities boast excellent urban infrastructures, close-knit communities, and beautiful parks and nature. Whether savoring the cherry blossoms in Kyoto or enjoying the fall foliage in Central Park, the distinct four seasons in both places allow for experiencing seasonal delicacies and engaging in activities unique to each time of the year. Moreover, the presence of a vibrant and condensed Japanese community in New York City adds to its appeal, providing a sense of comfort, connection, and support that I hope you will discover as well.

With my deep roots in the New York City lifestyle and understanding of its unique dynamics, I aim to share my knowledge, experiences, and insights to help guide you through the process of purchasing a co-op apartment. Together, let us make informed decisions that align with your lifestyle, financial goals, and aspirations. Join me on this journey as we explore the intricacies of cooperative ownership in the concrete jungle, embracing the dynamic energy, diverse culture, and limitless possibilities that the great city of New York has to offer.

CHAPTER 2

Co-op, Condo, and Renting

In this diverse landscape, it is essential to understand the distinctions in housing options between renting, co-ops, and condos. Let us delve into a comprehensive overview of these options, considering factors such as investment potential, pricing dynamics, and historical development.

RENTING:

Renting is a housing arrangement where individuals or families pay a monthly fee, known as rent, to occupy and use a property without owning it outright. Renting provides the flexibility to live in a desired location without the long-term commitment and responsibilities of ownership.

Renting an apartment in New York City has its own set of advantages and disadvantages. We will first start with the financial implications, considering the annual increase in rent expenses and the fact that rented apartments provide no equity. Let us look at the general pros and cons of renting.

Pros:

1. **Flexibility:** Renting provides the flexibility to easily move to different neighborhoods or cities, which is advantageous if your job or personal circumstances change.

2. **Lower responsibility:** As a renter, you are not responsible for the maintenance and repair costs, saving you both money and hassle.

3. **Amenities and services:** Rental buildings often come with amenities like gyms and laundry facilities, enhancing your overall living experience.

Cons:

1. **Rising rent expenses:** Renting in NYC comes with the drawback of increasing rent expenses annually, which can strain your budget and hinder saving for other financial goals.

2. **No equity:** Renting does not allow you to build equity; every payment goes to the landlord without accumulating ownership. This absence of equity means you will not have an asset to sell or use as collateral in the future.

3. **Limited control:** As a renter, you may face restrictions on significant modifications or personalizing the space, and decisions regarding lease renewals and potential rent increases are in the hands of the landlord.

To further illustrate the financial implications of renting in New York City, let's examine two examples with different rent amounts under an annual inflation of 5% (NYC 311, 2024), providing insights into the cumulative costs over three years.

Example 1: A studio apartment with a monthly rent of $3,000.

- Year 1: Monthly rent $3,000, annual rent expense $36,000

- Year 2: Monthly rent (5% inflation) $3,150, annual rent expense $37,800
- Year 3: Monthly rent (5% inflation) $3,308, annual rent expense $39,690

Over three years, the total rent expenses for this studio apartment would amount to approximately $113,490 with a 5% inflation and $108,000 without inflation.

Example 2: A one-bedroom apartment with a monthly rent of $4,000.

- Year 1: Monthly rent $4,000, annual rent expense $48,000
- Year 2: Monthly rent (5% inflation) $4,200, annual rent expense $50,400
- Year 3: Monthly rent (5% inflation) $4,410, annual rent expense $52,920

Over three years, the total rent expenses for this studio apartment would amount to approximately $151,320 with a 5% inflation and $144,000 without inflation. These simulations highlight the cumulative costs of renting over three years, considering an annual inflation rate of 5%. It is essential to note that landlords can arbitrarily increase rent prices beyond the 5% inflation annually, particularly if the rental property is not rent-stabilized.

In conclusion, renting in New York City provides flexibility and lower responsibility for maintenance, accompanied by access to amenities and services. However, the rise in rent expenses and the absence of equity are inevitable. Before deciding, evaluate your financial plans and circumstances to determine if renting aligns with your vision. I suggest you avoid automatically choosing to rent without considering other options.

CO-OP:

Cooperatives, commonly known as co-ops, have played a significant role in the New York City real estate landscape since the early 20th century (Cooperatornews, 2023). These housing arrangements emerged as an alternative to single-family homeownership, allowing residents to collectively own and manage entire buildings. A distinctive feature of co-ops is their stringent approval process, presenting challenges for foreign buyers like me. Co-op boards prioritize factors such as financial stability, references, and a commitment to the building's community. While foreign buyers may face additional scrutiny, thorough research and consultation can identify co-op buildings more open to international purchasers. In a co-op, ownership extends to a share of the entire building rather than a specific unit. The co-op management handles property tax payments on behalf of shareholders, providing documentation for individual tax return filings based on the respective share. Let us examine the pros and cons of being a co-op ownership.

Pros:

1. **Affordability:** Co-ops typically offer more affordable options compared to condo apartments, providing greater living space and quality for the same investment. Closing costs in co-op purchases are lower than those in condo purchases, contributing to overall financial stability and reduced foreclosure risks.

2. **Primary residence focus:** Co-ops are strictly for primary residence use. Residents enter this community-based setting through a rigorous board screening

process, fostering a peaceful and respectful living environment. This emphasis on primary residence distinguishes co-ops from condos, where owners often sublet units with less stringent screening.

3. **Community environment:** Co-ops cultivate a sense of community characterized by a family-friendly, neighborly atmosphere, and enhanced safety.

Cons:

1. **Higher down payment:** Co-op buyers typically face a higher initial deposit requirement, often exceeding 20% (Stevens, 2022). This significant upfront cost can strain budgets and pose challenges for saving toward other financial goals.

2. **Rigorous application process:** Purchasing a co-op involves a meticulous process, including a review of personal finances, credit history, board approval, and interviews with co-op board members. The strict scrutiny ensures alignment with the co-op building's requirements, and even if applicants are rejected, boards are not obligated to disclose the reasons.

3. **Restrictions:** Each co-op building has its own set of rules and policies, governing operations to maintain an optimal living community. These restrictions encompass subletting, home improvements, and other modifications, limiting the control residents have over personalizing their living space.

The subsequent financial illustration exemplifies the implications of co-op ownership in New York City, detailing a scenario with different rent amounts under an annual inflation rate of 5%. Homeowners can benefit from deductible tax expenses on property tax and mortgage interest when filing their tax return, resulting in a net annual payment lower than the gross annual payment over three years.

To illustrate how much owning a co-op apartment in New York City costs, we will examine a hypothetical scenario under an annual inflation rate of 5%. In the later chapters, we will delve into the details of the tax benefits that homeowners can leverage, including property tax and mortgage interest when filing their tax returns. This analysis aims to demonstrate that the net annual payment, after factoring in these tax benefits, is lower than the gross annual rent payment over three years.

Example: A studio apartment with a monthly payment of $3,000 (this includes a monthly maintenance fee of $1,200, and a monthly mortgage payment of $1,800.

Year 1: Annual payment after-tax benefits: $28,700

- Monthly maintenance fee: $1,200 + mortgage payment: $1,800 (totaling of $36,000 annually)
- Tax benefits: $7,300 (Considering a deductible tax expense of $19,200 with an approximate tax rate of 38% for New Yorkers (Smartasset, 2024))
  - Annual deductible tax expense: $19,200 (Includes property tax and mortgage interest). This amount is derived from a $7,200 annual property tax (12 months×$600, roughly half of the maintenance fee (Realty Collective, 2022)) and an annual mortgage interest of $12,000 (12 months × $1,000). 100% of interest on a mortgage is deductible up to $750,000 (IRS, 2024)).

Year 2: Annual payment after-tax benefits: $29,300

- Monthly maintenance fee: $1,260 (increased by +5% due to inflation) + mortgage payment: $1,800 (totaling of $36,720 annually)
- Tax benefits: $7,433 (Considering a deductible tax expense of $19,560 with an approximate tax rate of 38% for New Yorkers)
  - Annual deductible tax expense: $19,560 (Includes property tax and mortgage interest). This amount is derived from a $7,560 annual property tax (12 months × $630, roughly half of maintenance fee) and an annual mortgage interest of $12,000 (same as Year 1).

Year 3: After-tax annual payment: $29,900

- Monthly maintenance fee: $1,323 (increased by 5% due to inflation) + mortgage payment: $1,800 (totaling of $37,476 annually)
- Tax benefits: $7,576 (Considering a deductible tax expense of $19,938 with an approximate tax rate of 38% for New Yorkers)
  - Annual deductible tax expense: $19,938 (Includes property tax and mortgage interest). This amount is derived from a $7,938 annual property tax (12 months × $662, roughly half of maintenance fee) and an annual mortgage interest of $12,000 (same as Year 1).

Over the three-year period, the total net payment after tax benefits for a co-op studio apartment in this example will be approximately $87,900. This analysis highlights the financial benefits of owning a co-op in NYC. Despite excluding home equity for simplicity, owning a co-op yields lower payments compared to a three-year rental option of $113,490 discussed in the Rent section, thanks to tax advantages.

CONDO:

Condominiums, or condos, emerged in NYC in the 1960s as an alternative form of ownership (Cooperatornews, 2023). Unlike co-ops, condos grant individual ownership of specific units, which is often more appealing to foreign buyers and investors seeking flexibility and potential rental income. Condos tend to have fewer restrictions on subleasing, allowing owners to rent out their units more freely. This characteristic enhances their attractiveness for investment purposes and contributes to their higher purchase prices compared to co-ops. Additionally, condos are generally considered more liquid assets, as they can be bought and sold more easily without the extensive approval process associated with co-ops.

I have outlined key differences between condo and co-op apartments for those considering which option better suits their needs. It is highly recommended to grasp the concepts and purposes behind the establishment of both condos and co-ops to serve their respective owners.

- **Purchasing process:** The condominium purchasing process is shorter and simpler compared to the co-op's purchasing process. Co-op buyers are required to undergo the board's assessments of financial capabilities and interview processes to determine their fit within the co-op apartment community.

- **Pricing:** Typically, condo apartments are more expensive than co-op apartments. This is mostly due to the flexibility in how the apartment can be used, either for living or renting out. The limited inventory of condos in New York City also contributes to higher prices.

- **Flexibility:** A condo owner is granted physical ownership of the apartment unit, unlike a co-op owner who owns shares in the entire building. A condo owner has full control over how the unit is used, whether for personal living or subleasing from the first day of ownership.

- **Living environment:** On the brighter side of the rigorous screening process for co-op owners, there is more assurance about the quality of neighbors. As co-op residents primarily use their units for residential purposes, a friendly and peaceful living environment is more common. In contrast, condos offer the flexibility of renting out without a screening process, resulting in a wider range of people in terms of demographics, backgrounds, and lifestyles.

While this book focuses on the co-op apartment purchasing process without equally delving into condo purchasing process, I still recommend readers going for a condo purchase to continue reading this book to educate yourself on making the most of each condo and co-op ownership.

In addition to co-ops and condos, although with limited inventory, there are "condoops," which combine aspects of both ownership types. Condoops can have cooperative elements, such as a board approval process and community regulations, while also allowing for individual ownership and more flexible subleasing options. They offer a unique middle ground between co-ops and condos, appealing to buyers who desire a mix of community and flexibility.

Understanding the nuances of each housing option will empower you to make an informed decision aligned with your preferences and financial goals. In the following Chapter 3, you will explore an overview of factors surrounding purchasing, such as mortgage interest rates, subleasing options, and more. Chapters 4 and 5 will delve deeper into all associated costs of co-op purchase and co-op market research. Chapter 6 reviews a step-by-step process of what to expect in a co-op purchase, followed by my own experience. Lastly, Chapter 7 wraps up the book by reviewing how we should maintain our mindsets post-purchase.

CHAPTER 3

Purchasing an Apartment in NYC

We will now delve into the types of costs associated with owning a co-op and other factors to consider when deciding whether to purchase. We will also discuss the actual steps involved, highlight the differences between co-ops and condos, and review some related topics to get started.

INTEREST ON MORTGAGE:

First, we will discuss one of the largest expenses of purchasing a co-op apartment: the cost of borrowing, if you are planning to take out a mortgage. With the Federal Reserve raising interest rates in 2022 and 2023, the cost of borrowing a mortgage has continued increasing, causing concern among prospective home buyers. This trend has implications for the housing market, specifically on the borrowing rate for a home mortgage.

Let us review how interest on a mortgage works. The mortgage interest rate is impacted by the Federal Reserve's monetary policy and the yield on the "10-year US treasury bond" (Brookings, 2023). The "10-year US treasury bond" is considered a benchmark for long-term interest rates and serves as a "risk-free rate" in the financial markets. The "risk-free rate" signifies the return an investor would expect from an investment without the risk of default, backed by the U.S. government that has never defaulted.

Banks, such as mortgage lenders, carefully track fluctuations in the risk-free rate and establish their mortgage interest rates by adding a margin into the risk-free rate. When these banks lend mortgage funds to borrowers, this margin, also called yield spread premium, will be the lender's profit in exchange for default risks of borrowers, operating costs, and administrative fees. Banks also make a profit from loan origination and closing fees which include application charges, underwriting fees, and more.

Typically, lenders assess the borrower's credit risk to determine the margin they will apply. Borrowers with stronger credit profiles, who are considered less risky, may be offered a lower margin, while those with higher credit risk may face a higher margin. Lenders also consider their own profitability goals and market competitiveness when determining the margin percentage.

We can get an idea of the range of margin percentages from the historical data and market trends. In the past, mortgage lenders have commonly added their margins ranging from 1% to 3% above the prevailing risk-free rate (Bankrate, 2024). However, it is important to note that these figures are not definitive and can vary significantly depending on the lender and prevailing market conditions.

HOW INTEREST RATE AFFECTS THE HOUSING MARKET:

Interest rates play a pivotal role in the housing market. Lower interest rates reduce borrowing costs, making homeownership more affordable and potentially increasing the demand for homes. Conversely, rising interest rates elevate borrowing costs, potentially reducing affordability, and suppressing demand. When interest rates rise, resulting in decreased buyer demand and less competitive bidding scenarios, sellers may need to adjust their pricing strategy, such as lowering sale prices to attract buyers in a higher-rate environment. Conversely, decreasing interest rates can stimulate buyer demand and purchasing power, potentially leading to an uptick in home prices.

I would like to emphasize here that even if you purchase your apartment during a period of higher interest rates, the cost of borrowing can potentially be mitigated through "refinancing" after the purchase. "Refinancing" allows you to secure a new loan at a new interest rate, potentially reducing your monthly mortgage payments when interest rates decrease. This can result in long-term savings and improved affordability. On the other hand, the home price cannot be adjusted after purchasing. This concept suggests that purchasing an apartment during a high-interest period, with the prospect of future refinancing if sellers list their homes at lower prices to entice buyers, might be a viable strategy.

Additionally, tax benefits associated with interest on a mortgage are another advantage for homeowners. We will delve into refinancing and tax deductibility in detail later, but this aspect further adds to the financial considerations when assessing the purchasing or renting.

While interest rate hikes can impact home prices, it is essential to recognize that various factors contribute to the dynamics of the real estate market. Supply and demand, economic conditions, and buyer sentiment all play crucial roles in shaping home prices. By considering the potential benefits of refinancing and the tax deductibility of mortgage expenses, buyers can make informed decisions regarding their homeownership journey.

SUBLETTING:

Throughout your life journey, circumstances may arise where considering subletting becomes a viable option. This might happen when you get married and expand your family, face temporary relocation due to work or personal reasons, undergo financial challenges, or evaluate market conditions that render selling less favorable. In contrast to condos, where owners can sublet from day one, co-op buildings have unique subletting policies, designed primarily for primary residences rather than investment properties. Nevertheless, co-op buildings permit subletting under specific conditions and requirements. If your co-op allows subletting, and you and your potential sub-tenant meet the necessary criteria, subletting your co-op apartment will be an option.

It is important to grasp that subletting in a co-op is generally subject to specific limitations and guidelines. These guidelines exist to preserve the cooperative nature of the building and ensure that most residents are owner-occupiers. Each co-op building has its set of rules and restrictions regarding subletting, which you should thoroughly review and comply with before contemplating subletting your unit.

For instance, a typical condition for subleasing in a co-op might require you to have been a resident owner-occupier for a certain number of years before becoming eligible to sublet your unit. This requirement aims to maintain the cooperative nature of the building by ensuring that owners have a genuine commitment to the community before allowing subleasing.

Other conditions may include restrictions on the duration of subleases, the number of subleases allowed within a specific period, and the approval process for selecting sub-tenants. It is crucial to acquaint yourself with these conditions and understand the obligations and responsibilities that come with subletting your co-op. During my search for a co-op apartment, I consistently paid attention to the flexibility of the subleasing policy in the co-op building and the number of years of residency required before subletting. Discussing the specific sublet policy with your broker during viewings is also vital. Based on my experience, it was not rare to find co-op apartments on sale that allow permanent subletting after living two years. If your co-op building's policy does not allow sublets, you might end up needing to sell your apartment when you move to another home.

By adhering to the guidelines and requirements set forth by your co-op building, you can explore the possibility of subletting your unit if it aligns with your specific needs and circumstances. It is always advisable to consult your co-op board or management to ensure you understand about the subletting process and any potential implications. Simultaneously, approaching subletting with a conservative mindset is crucial, as co-op ownership is primarily for owner-occupancy.

HOME APPRECIATION

While there are no guarantees, historically, New York City real estate has shown resilience and the potential for continuous growth. In general, your home payments consist of three components: home principal, mortgage interest, and building maintenance and common area fees. As you continue paying down the home principal, the accumulated balance of your home principal payment becomes your home equity, contributing to your net worth. This home equity is subject to market appreciation, while mortgage interest and home maintenance payments are the costs associated with owning the home.

The longer you own it, the more it grows. I would suggest that the optimal duration of ownership, in terms of home equity growth, is permanent or if you can manage ownership with a combination of uses, including your own living space, your family members' residential use, and potential sublets. Alternatively, you could view your monthly home equity payment as if you were putting your cash aside for a low-yield conservative instrument such as a certificate of deposit, high-yield savings account, or US Treasury bonds, but you can receive the physical benefit of living there.

In addition to home equity growth, you are effectively locking in your monthly cash outflow on your property upon signing the purchase contract. This could be excellent news, especially considering the trajectory of rising rent especially in New York City. If you are renting a property that is not rent-stabilized, your rent could easily increase by 3% to 10% annually.

While the growth rate may not match that of the U.S. stock market, the home equity you build benefits from the appreciation of the real estate market. In contrast, when you rent, there is no equity-building component, and the entire payment is akin to an expense.

TANGIBLE BENEFIT:

Accumulating financial equity over time through property ownership also provides tangible benefits that typical low-yield financial investment products never offer. While your home equity appreciates, you can physically live in the space, enjoying the benefits of owning a property such as personalizing your living space, making improvements, and taking pride in homeownership, which you could feel a different kind of satisfaction compared to investing in stocks, where ownership is more abstract. Since you need a place to live anyway, it naturally makes sense to allocate a portion of your financial portfolio to a real estate for your primary residence.

LEARNING THORUGH EXPERIENCES:

I can guarantee that the earlier you buy real estate in your life, the smarter you will get as you will be more educated and be able to act in each moment. It will give you a great kickstart for your personal finance and accumulate your net worth with a portion of your portfolio in real estate.

I also experienced that despite the positive aspects of home purchasing, it is common to feel overwhelmed and experience "home buyer's remorse." In my hindsight, this emotional journey is natural to have, considering the magnitude of the decision. Personalizing your experience and sharing it with a select few can ease the stress associated with such a substantial financial commitment.

The first home purchase, often the most expensive in one's life, can trigger anxieties. Questions like whether the apartment is too expensive, the neighborhood is the best choice, or if it is the right time to buy can arise. Overcoming these doubts involves thorough self-reflection and understanding your long-term vision. Educating oneself by visiting multiple properties, consulting professionals, and learning from others' experiences is key. While buyer's remorse is common, strategic learning and consideration can lead to a satisfying and convincing decision.

MAKING INFORMED DECISIONS:

To make informed investment decisions, start by assessing your current financial situation and comparing it with the difference between your existing rent payment and the fees associated with owning an apartment. It is important to note that these fees do not include your home equity payment, which can accumulate as your asset rather than a pure expense. Evaluating your budget, encompassing the down payment, monthly mortgage payments, maintenance fees, and other expenses, will provide a clearer understanding of what you can comfortably afford.

I advise against utilizing your W-2 income raise and bonus for financial planning. Instead, maintain a conservative approach in your planning, considering that your income remains stable at the very least. Consider potential scenarios, including health issues that may interrupt your ability to work, and assess your capacity to sustain payments. Co-ops often mandate "post-closing liquid assets" as part of the co-op board assessment to validate your financial strength (we will review in detail later).

CHAPTER 4

Cost of Ownership

In this chapter, we will delve into the financial intricacies associated with the cost of being a co-op owner. As you gear up for homeownership, it is important that you under understand the various expenses, ranging from closing costs, monthly maintenance fees, and mortgage payment. Additionally, we will touch on how tax benefits impact your net expenses.

The breakdown below illustrates a simplified example including both monthly and closing costs with a $420,000 co-op apartment with a requirement of a 20% down payment and a 30-years mortgage at the rate of 6% interest. We will review each component in detail as well as other financial responsibilities along with a coop ownership:

Monthly payment: $3,200 (maintenance fees + mortgage payment)

1. **Maintenance fees: $1,200**

   - Property taxes: $600 (deductible on your taxable income)
   - Other expenses: $600

2. **Mortgage payment: $2,000**

   - Mortgage principal: $1,000

- Mortgage interest: $1,000 (deductible on your taxable income)

3. **Closing costs: $9,000**

- Attorney fees: $3,000
- Mortgage application fees: $3,000
- Coop application service fees: $3,000

MAINTENANCE FEES:

A recurring cost of co-op ownership, the monthly maintenance fee, represents various fees, including property taxes, building maintenance and repairs, utilities, trash, staff salaries, and insurance. The maintenance fees can vary significantly depending on the co-op building. For example, with a $420,000 co-op apartment, the monthly maintenance fee could range from roughly $800 to $2,000 or more. Generally, apartments with higher maintenance fees offer higher quality, renovated units, and better building amenities. On the side note, maintenance fees are subject to inflation as these fees sustain the building operations. Budgeting for potential increases is advisable when assessing co-op affordability.

In New York City, property taxes are typically part of the monthly maintenance fee, constituting around 50% of the total (Realty Collective, 2022) and the co-op management pays property taxes from the maintenance fees collected from the owners. You are responsible for the amount based on your share of property tax, determined by your unit's size and value.

In this example, assuming 50% of the $1,200 monthly maintenance fee covers property taxes, $600 contributes to property taxes. Property tax is deductible on your taxable income when filing your 1040 individual tax return. After the calendar year, the co-op management issues Form 1098, detailing the property tax per share. Each co-op owner calculates your portion of property taxes based on the number of shares of their unit and the property tax paid by the co-op management per share, inputting that amount on Schedule A of their 1040 tax form.

MORTGAGE PAYMENT:

If you take on a mortgage your apartment purchase, a portion of your mortgage payment will be allocated to interest. In our example, assuming a mortgage loan of $336,000 (80% of a $420,000 apartment), the monthly mortgage payment is $2,000, covering both the mortgage principal (home equity) and mortgage interest.

It is important to note that in your mortgage payment, for example $2,000, a majority portion goes toward mortgage interest at the early stage of the loan term. In other words, as you continue paying off a monthly mortgage of $2,000, you gradually pay off a larger sum of your home's principal, resulting in a lower amount going toward mortgage interest. For instance, your first year's mortgage payment consists of $1,300 of mortgage interest and $700 of home principal, while your second year's mortgage payment comprises $1,400 of mortgage interest and $600 of home principal.

Related to the interest expense on a mortgage, a question that may arise as we continue paying off the mortgage is whether to pay off the principal early, as it can save you on interest. This decision depends on your investment risk tolerance, and you should weigh whether it is more beneficial to save on mortgage interest or invest your cash in other opportunities for profit. However, beyond finance, achieving the non-financial satisfaction of reducing the principal and attaining a sense of financial freedom can provide significant emotional benefits. The stress related to your personal finances should not be overlooked in the long term. We all need to evaluate this decision based on both financial and non-financial aspects.

TAX BENEFITS:

In addition to property taxes, mortgage interest provides another tax benefit for apartment owners. The US government offers incentives to recognize the crucial role of homeownership in building stable communities and fostering economic growth. By permitting homeowners to deduct property taxes and mortgage interest from their taxable income, the government encourages individuals to invest in their homes and fortify local neighborhoods.

There is a ceiling amount for tax deduction on both property taxes and mortgage interest. As of 2024, you can claim a property tax deduction of up to $10,000 ($5,000 if you're married and filing separately) and a mortgage interest deduction up to $750,000 for both single and married taxpayers (IRS, 2024).

In our previous example, we had a monthly maintenance fee of $1,200, with $600 allocated to property taxes (resulting in annual property taxes of $7,200). Additionally, a monthly mortgage interest of $1,200 accumulates to an annual interest of $12,000. It becomes evident that we quickly reach the property tax deduction cap while being able to deduct a significantly high amount of interest expenses from taxable income.

Let us delve into a little more detail of these tax benefits with actual numbers and compare them with a renting situation, where what you pay is purely an expense without building home equity.

Cost of Ownership

If you live in New York City, the combined state and city tax rate would be approximately 36% when you file the 1040 individual income tax. Most of you would probably opt for the standard tax deduction over the itemized deduction if you were not a homeowner, given that the standard deduction (in 2024, single: $14,600, married couples filing jointly $29,200) exceeds the itemized deduction that you can include as tax deductions (IRS, 2024).

Now, as a homeowner with a home priced at $420,000 using the same example, you would select the itemized deduction as you can claim deductible expenses of $19,200 (a property tax of $7,200 and a mortgage interest of $12,000). On the 1040 form, subtracting this deduction from your gross income reduces your taxable net income, resulting in tax benefits of approximately $6,900 (36% of $19,200).

Given the example above, we can calculate your actual out-of-pocket expenses and the net cost of owning a co-op apartment after tax benefits. The annual expense of maintenance fee and mortgage interest from the example is $26,400 (annual maintenance fee of $14,400 and mortgage expense of $12,000), and the tax benefits after the state and city tax rate is $6,900.

After subtracting the tax benefit amount based on New York City's tax rate, the annual net housing expenses will be $19,500 (monthly $1,650), which represents your annual housing cost. Meanwhile, your annual cash payment totals $38,400 (monthly $3,200). Also, keep in your mind that your annual mortgage payment of $24,000 (monthly $2,000) includes a home principal portion of $12,000 (monthly $1,000), which constitutes your home equity.

If we were to convert the homeowner's net expense of $19,500 into a renting scenario, it would equate to securing a rental apartment for $1,650 per month. Considering the quality and space typically available for such a rental price in New York City, owning an apartment emerges as a highly advantageous choice.

It's essential to understand your cash outflow by differentiating between sole expenses, tax benefits, and home equity. In addition to the positive aspect of weighing net co-op expenses versus rental expenses, remember that your rent expense is also subject to inflation over the years while you can fix a mortgage payment (once again, the maintenance fee is also subject to annual inflation adjustment). Although this simulation shows how tax benefits work and the bright side of the net expense of homeownership, you still need to ensure that you can make a monthly cash payment.

CLOSING COSTS:

We will continue using the same example of a home priced at $420,000 for simulating the closing cost calculation. As a rule of thumb, closing costs typically fall in the range of 1.5% to 3% of the home price, which would amount to somewhere between $6,300 to $12,600 (Hauseit, 2024). During the closing process, you could expect the following items within the price range.

1. **Attorney fees: $3,000**

   - Attorney legal fee $2,000 (50% payable upon hiring an attorney after your offer is accepted by the seller), contract and closing document preparation $500, due diligence report $300, and other miscellaneous fees $200.

2. **Mortgage application fees: $3,000**

- Underwriting fee $1,000, appraisal fee $1,000, and other miscellaneous fees $1,000

3. **Co-op application service fees: $3,000**

   - Application fees $1,000, financing fee $500, co-op attorney fee of $500, move-in fee $500, and other administrative processing fees $500.

In contrast, using the same example of a home sale price of $420,000, let's highlight some of the closing costs that sellers, not buyers, must pay just for your future reference. In general, sellers have to bear higher closing costs compared to what buyers owe, suggesting that entering into a buying transaction is easier in terms of a housing transaction. Using the same example with the $420,000 apartment, the following percentages for the seller's closing costs would be applied based on a rule of thumb in New York City (Prevu, 2024).

- NY broker commission: 6% or $25,200
- NY city transfer tax: 1% or $4,200
- Attorney fee: 0.7% or $2,940
- NY state transfer tax: 0.4% or $1,680

In addition to the above, sellers should remember the capital gain tax on potential sale profit. The good news is that the seller can exclude taxable capital gain up to $250,000 (or $500,000 if married filing jointly) if the home meets exclusion eligibility criteria (IRS, Capital gain exclusion, 2024). These eligibility tests include, for example, whether it was used as a primary residence, owned for over two years in the last five-year period, no previous claims of this exclusion in the past two years, not purchased through a like-kind exchange, and not subject to expatriation tax provisions (apply to U.S. citizens who have given up their citizenship and long-term residents who have given up their U.S. residency status as a result of living abroad for an extended period).

TYPES OF MORTGAGES:

Now, let's discuss the different types of mortgages. Typically, you will choose either a fixed-rate or adjustable-rate mortgage (ARM) that better suits your payment plan based on your risk tolerance. Before you apply for a mortgage, it's crucial to shop around with multiple lenders to find the best rates and terms. In this section, we will discuss the details of fixed-rate and adjustable-rate mortgages, and in the following section, we will review how different mortgage terms impact your mortgage payment.

1. **Fixed-rate mortgage:** With a fixed-rate mortgage, the interest rate remains constant throughout the loan term, providing stability and predictability. This is ideal if you prefer a consistent monthly payment over the long run. Given the nature of fixing the rate, you are protected from potential rate increases and provided with a secured monthly payment. However, the interest rate of a fixed-rate mortgage is typically higher than an adjustable-rate mortgage. Fixed-rate mortgages are usually available for different loan terms, such as 15 years and 30 years.

2. **Adjustable-rate mortgage (ARM):** An adjustable-rate mortgage offers an initial fixed-rate period, typically lasting 3, 5, 7, or 10 years, after which the interest rate adjusts periodically based on market conditions, potentially moving higher or lower. Adjustable-rate mortgage plan usually offers lower rates in the initial fixed rate period compared to fixed-rate mortgages,

making them attractive for borrowers who plan to sell or refinance before the rate adjustment period.

It would make sense to select a fixed rate when the market is experiencing lower interest rates, such as in early 2021 due to the effects of COVID-19, to secure your mortgage rate for a longer period. If it's unlikely that the interest rate will decrease further, then selecting an adjustable-rate mortgage wouldn't be logical. However, during a year with higher rates, like in 2023 when the Federal Reserve raised its benchmark rate 11 consecutive times, you would probably want to consider refinancing your loan after several years. In such cases, it would make more sense to choose an adjustable-rate mortgage (ARM) which offers a lower initial fixed rate compared to a traditional fixed-rate mortgage. Although there would be no guarantee, if the rate decreases within the initial fixed-rate period of your ARM contract, you can refinance to secure a lower rate.

Additionally, let us quickly review different size of the mortgage.

1. **Regular (conventional) mortgage:** Most buyers fall into this loan category, except for those who buy high-value homes with Jumbo loans or take government-backed loans. In New York City for 2024, a loan amount under $1,149,825 is a regular loan and exceeding this limit falls into a Jumbo loan (The Mortgage Reports, 2023).

2. **Jumbo Loan:** This loan poses a higher risk to lenders due to their larger size, they usually require a higher credit score and come with slightly higher interest rates compared to regular mortgages.

3. **Government-backed loans:** Offered by government agencies including the Federal Housing Administration

(FHA), Veterans Affairs (VA), or the United States Department of Agriculture (USDA). These loans will save you mortgage interest and down payment.

- FHA loan: Offers a limited loan amount while allowing you to buy a home with a credit score as low as 580 and a down payment of 3.5% (HUD, 2024). This loan requires a borrower to pay for mortgage insurance premiums that hedge against the borrower's default.

- USDA loan: Requires lower mortgage insurance requirements and can allow you to buy a home without a down payment. You must meet income requirements and buy a home in an eligible rural area (Midland States Bank, 2024).

- VA loan: Allows you to buy a home with no down payment and lower interest rates than most other types of loans. You must meet veterans' service requirements in the Armed Forces or National Guard to qualify (Midland States Bank, 2024).

LOAN TERM:

When applying for mortgage loans, you need to choose the term on your mortgage, each option offering different monthly payments and interest rates. Shorter loan term involves higher monthly payments but lower interest rates due to the shorter risk exposure for lenders. Despite higher monthly payments, shorter term saves on overall interest costs and build home equity quickly.

Let's compare two examples with different terms. As more people are opting for adjustable-rate mortgages (ARM) rather than fixed-rate loans in 2024, amidst record-high mortgage rates, we will use two adjustable-rate mortgages (30-year loans) with initial fixed-rate periods of 7 and 10 years. After these periods, rates will adjust to market rates. Suppose you're considering a $336,000 mortgage at 6% for the 7-year ARM and 6.25% for the 10-year ARM.

- A 7-year ARM with an initial interest rate of 6%, with a 30-year term
  - Monthly principal payment of $1,000
  - Interest payment of $1,000 (until the 7th year). Interest expense for the first 7 years will be $84,000.
- A 10-year ARM with an initial interest rate of 6.25%, with a 30-year term
  - Monthly principal payment of $1,000
  - Interest payment of $1,050 (until 10th year). Interest expense for the first 7 years will be $88,200.

Opting for the 7-year ARM could save you about $50 monthly compared to the 10-year ARM during the initial 7 years, though it carries the risk of earlier rate adjustments. Refinancing may be an option if rates move in your favor, reducing overall interest expenses. With the 10-year ARM, you get 3 more years of fixed-rate stability, paying slightly more interest over the initial 7 years (around $6,200 more). However, shorter mortgage periods generally result in lower interest expenses if you can afford a higher monthly cash payment.

REFINANCE:

Refinancing your mortgage can save you money on interest expenses, making it an appealing option. It allows borrowers to leverage favorable market conditions, such as lower interest rates, to enhance their overall mortgage repayment situation. On the other hand, banks benefit from refinancing by maintaining relationships with borrowers, sustain interest income, and potentially cross-sell other financial products and services.

For example, let's say you bought a $420,000 apartment with a 20% down payment, leaving you with a $336,000 mortgage. Your current 30-year fixed-rate mortgage is at 6%. However, after 2 years, interest rates drop, and you find a lender offering 4% for a new 30-year term. Currently, you're paying $1,000 in monthly interest, but with the lower rate, it could drop to $600, saving you $400 each month. Over time, these savings can really add up.

The cost of refinancing includes application fees, appraisal fees, title search fees, and closing costs. Generally, refinancing ranges from 2% to 5% of the new loan amount. For instance, if your remaining mortgage balance is $300,000, expect costs between $6,000 and $15,000. You want to consider how quickly you can recover these costs compared to potential monthly savings to reach the breakeven point. For example, if your refinance costs $6,000 and you save $400 monthly, it'll take 15 months to break even. Ideally, aim for a breakeven period of around 15 months.

In general, you are going to have two payment options: pay fees upfront or roll them into your new loan. While including costs in the loan spreads expenses but increases your mortgage balance and monthly payments, paying upfront may save on interest in the long run if you have the funds. You can decide which payment option to choose based on your funding and payment plan. The refinancing process usually takes about 30 to 45 days and involves providing financial documents like income verification and tax returns. Keeping an eye on interest rates and refinance options is key to potential cost savings. If this effort results in cost savings, the time invested would be worthwhile.

POST-CLOSING LIQUIDITY:

Another important aspect in the purchasing process if a "post-closing liquidity" requirement which refers to funds available after purchasing a co-op. These assets act as a safety net, showing your ability to handle expenses and emergencies. Co-op boards often require proof of post-purchase liquid assets to ensure financial stability. Demonstrating sufficient post-closing assets reassures the board of your financial responsibility. This protects both the co-op and individual owners, ensuring long-term financial health.

For example, with a $420,000 home and 20% down payment, your total monthly payment, including mortgage and maintenance fees, would be around $3,200. This means you need $76,800 (2 years of payments) in post-closing liquidity. In total, for you to be qualified as a buyer, you'd need to save at minimum of $169,200 (a down payment of $84,000, closing costs of $8,400 or 2% of the home price, and a post-closing liquidity requirement of $76,800) in this example. All assets must be supported by official documents reviewed by the co-op. The board may also require additional financial information if your assets are just above their requirements. I advise all buyers understand these financing requirements to be fully prepared for a smooth co-op application process.

Sometimes, the board requests an emergency fund deposit to address potential financial challenges. This request is not uncommon, especially if your assets' value is just above the board's financial requirements after the post-closing liquidity assessment. For instance, the co-op board may require a deposit kept in an escrow account equivalent to 1 to 2 years' worth of maintenance fees. This deposit serves as a safeguard if you face financial difficulties and cannot pay monthly fees. Typically, the board releases this deposit to you after 2 to 3 years if you have not defaulted on payment for monthly maintenance fees.

Using the same housing example, if the board asks for a 2-year deposit ($1,200 for 24 months totaling $28,800), you need at least $198,200 (additional deposit request of $28,800, post-closing liquidity of $76,800, a down payment of $84,000, and estimated closing costs of $8,400 or 2% of the home price) to proceed.

In some cases, co-op boards allow gifting from family members to cover the deposit. Official documentation, including a gift letter and supporting financial records, is required. Post-closing assets must be easily convertible to cash, excluding assets like real estate or restricted retirement accounts.

SUMMARY:

We delved into monthly maintenance fees, property taxes, closing costs, and mortgage interest with refinancing options, uncovering valuable insights to aid in your budgeting and financial planning. One crucial aspect that should not be overlooked is the need for a cushion of two years' worth of liquid assets. This serves as a safeguard, ensuring you can confidently meet your monthly expenses and have a financial buffer in case unforeseen circumstances arise. By demonstrating your ability to maintain this level of financial stability, you can enhance your chances of being accepted by the co-op board.

It's important to note that the costs and benchmarks used in my examples are for illustrative purposes only, and actual costs may vary depending on market conditions and related regulations. It is advisable to simulate your own costs to gain a deeper understanding of your financial obligations or consult with professionals who specialize in co-op ownership. Conduct thorough research based on your unique circumstances for accurate planning.

CHAPTER 5

Researching Process

This chapter aims to guide you through the research process, equipping you with the knowledge and considerations necessary to make informed choices. By understanding your financial capabilities, exploring the market, evaluating co-op quality, and considering various factors that contribute to your ideal living experience, you can navigate this process with confidence and find a co-op apartment that aligns with your needs and goals.

I do want to emphasis that patience is key during this research period, especially if you're new to the market. While a seemingly perfect deal may suddenly appear, it's important to stay calm and exercise caution. Without a solid understanding of the market and available inventory, you need to maintain control and be a smart buyer. Remember, you're making a decision that will impact the next several years to decades of owning an apartment. Building conviction takes time and a well-informed approach.

Based on my own experience, I found that my budget and apartment features and options changed multiple times since the beginning of the research and viewing. It's a gradual process of viewing homes outside your price range and those that fall short of your living standards, which ultimately leads you to discover the optimal and comfortable search target. These experiences make you smarter and more convinced of what you are looking for in an apartment within your budget.

BUDGETING:

Before coming up with your budget for your first apartment, take the time to thoroughly assess your financial situation. Consider factors such as your monthly income, current debt repayment schedules, cash reserves for immediate needs (around five months' worth of your monthly spending), down payment capabilities, post-closing liquidity, closing costs, and whether you plan to purchase with someone else (family, etc.). Understanding these financial boundaries and possibilities will help you establish a realistic budget and refine your research process.

As you understand your financial situation, you also need to comprehend the real estate market and be familiar with the quality of apartments each city can offer to establish your budget. This budget is influenced by various factors, including your financial capabilities, mortgage financing limits, and desired level of affordability.

In my experience, I started by setting rough price ranges from $350,000 to $500,000 while projecting monthly cash payments and financing options. Next, I made appointments to view apartments within this price range to understand the value and quality of apartments available at various price points. I encourage you to set your mind that these viewings are just for your budgeting and understanding the market and not for making an offer. Throughout the initial viewing process, my perception of the market and budget evolved gradually. I started having a solid idea of how much money can offer what quality of apartment in NYC. I eventually settled on a budget range from $400,000 to $450,000 for a studio apartment. This amount allowed for a comfortable living arrangement within my financial means. While a $500,000 apartment may have offered nice and more features, I found that a $450,000 budget struck a balance between a comfortable living space and an optimal financial journey.

REFINING YOUR RESEARCH:

After determining your budget, take further steps to refine your research on the neighborhood and apartment amenities you are looking for. Understanding your desired neighborhood and lifestyle preferences is vital. Research and visit different areas to assess transportation options, proximity to schools, availability of parking, and nearby amenities such as parks, restaurants, and shopping centers. Assessing these characteristics in relation to your lifestyle will help you narrow down your neighborhood options.

I had a decent idea of how it feels to live in Manhattan, Brooklyn, and Queens, making it not difficult for me to choose the Upper East Side as the neighborhood where I wanted to purchase an apartment. I am a fan of the deep cultural vibes of the upper side of Manhattan, the walkability to the city, the quieter and family-oriented environment, and the proximity to Central Park. While Brooklyn was an option due to its lower maintenance fees and family-friendly spaces with plenty of parks and activities, I preferred not to rely on frequent transportation to get to Manhattan.

In terms of apartment amenities, make sure to repeatedly ask yourself about the priorities of amenities unless your budget is unlimited. Typical apartment amenities in NYC include a doorman, washer/dryer, elevator, outdoor space, gym, lounge/library, and more, and these are always nice to have; however, you do have to pay a premium that increases your monthly maintenance and amenity fees. Additionally, make sure to write down your priorities for the features in your apartment unit. Ask yourself how important it is to have a spacious kitchen space, natural sunlight, any specific layout preferences, and whether you would prefer a higher or lower floor.

I did not want any extra amenities that I do not need except for a part-time or full-time doorman and laundry facility inside the building. While it would be great to have common recreational spaces, an indoor gym, and barbecue space, these would inevitably increase your monthly fees regardless of whether you use them. Knowing my priorities, I had a clear vision when searching for an apartment.

I also prioritized a comfortable kitchen space and natural sunlight during the daytime. I skipped apartment listings that faced another building and had blocked views. I was specifically looking for the alcove studio structure instead of a straight shape, as it provided a larger impression of the unit. Overall, I avoided old and damaged units. By physically visiting several units, it helped me develop a keen eye for evaluating the condition of walls, floors, kitchens, and bathrooms. The more time you spend visiting apartments and thinking through your preferences, the more certain you can be about whether you want to make an offer for a particular apartment.

CO-OP FEES & POLICIES:

Maintenance fees and policies associated with co-op apartments require careful evaluation. Assess the level of monthly maintenance fees and understand what is included, such as utilities or common area upkeep. Additionally, review the co-op's policies on subletting, gifting, and co-purchasing to ensure they align with your plans and provide the desired flexibility.

I aimed to keep maintenance fees as low as reasonably possible, ranging from the lower end of $1,000 to the higher end of $1,500 if other specifications were attractive. Maintenance fees are pure expenses that do not contribute to accumulating home equity. Although approximately 50% of maintenance fees covers property taxes, can reduce your tax, it is still preferable to maintain reasonable maintenance fees.

Another important factor to consider is the co-op's subletting policy as having an option to sublet the apartment offers valuable opportunities for building assets. By renting out the apartment, your tenants can contribute to the principal and mortgage payments, while you can still receive tax benefits as a homeowner. This option is especially beneficial if you foresee the need for a larger home in the future, such as when getting married or starting a family. It serves as a valuable filter to consider, allowing you to explore the possibility of renting out the apartment rather than selling it.

By carefully evaluating maintenance fees and subletting policies, you can ensure that your decision aligns with your financial goals and provides flexibility for potential life changes. This consideration contributes to overall satisfaction and long-term financial well-being as a co-op owner.

I cannot stress enough the importance of spending at least six months on your co-op search, both online and physically visiting units while engaging in conversations with several brokers. This extended period will educate you about your optimal budgeting and develop a keen eye for evaluating unit conditions. The more time you spend, the more confident you will build in identifying what you want and what you don't need, allowing you to eliminate unnecessary features that may increase your cash outflow. Resist the urge to immediately jump at attractive units; let them pass, knowing that you will likely encounter similar listings. Keep in mind that this initial search process is not for making an offer, but rather about educating yourself.

CHAPTER 6

Purchasing Process

This chapter will cover most of the co-op purchase processes as you finally decided to make an offer to buy. It includes making an offer, hiring an attorney for due diligence on the property, applying for a mortgage, and preparing for the board package and interview. As you will be involved in signing a variety of contracts such as purchasing contract, mortgage contract, and others in these processes, you should be familiar with these major processes to execute them in a timely manner.

1. MAKING AN OFFER:

Let's say you visited 5 to 10 apartments and you are finally convinced that you found an apartment you like and want to put on an offer to the seller. This offer usually includes the proposed purchase price and any specific terms you would like to include.

When making an offer on a co-op apartment, it is customary to include a few important documents along with your offer. These documents help demonstrate your financial qualifications and it indicates you are a serious buyer. Typically, you will need to submit your mortgage pre-approval letter issued by a mortgage lender and that states the maximum loan amount you are qualified for based on your income, creditworthiness, and other factors. This pre-approval serves as proof that you can obtain financing for the purchase. To clarify, you don't have to go with this pre-approved mortgage with this specific lender, but it will give an assurance for seller's broker, seller, and co-op management that you are a qualified buyer.

Additionally, you are most likely requested by a seller's broker to provide a draft of your personal financial statement, which the Excel format should be provided. This personal statement outlines your monthly income, financial assets, debts, and the home purchase deposit you are planning to put down for your offer. Including these documents allows the broker and the seller to review your preliminary qualification for the co-op transaction, giving them confidence in your ability to secure the necessary financing and move forward with the application process.

In my experience, if you show an interest in making an offer, the broker will typically tell you an estimated minimum net assets after debt and monthly income to determine if you are eligible for the board's acceptance in terms of finance status. Ultimately, these conversations with various brokers further help me stay informed regarding the numerous factors going into purchasing a co-op.

2. NEGOTIATION:

The seller may accept your offer as is, or they may counter with a different price or terms. Negotiations continue until both parties reach a mutual agreement on the purchase price and contract terms.

It's important to recognize that there are often other buyers who also consider it one of the best options within their budget range. In the co-op market, negotiations on the purchase price are typically limited compared to condos or homes. Co-ops usually have set prices determined by the board or the seller, leaving little room for negotiation.

However, there are other factors that can make your offer more appealing to the seller, such as the type of offer you present. One significant distinction is between a cash offer and a mortgage offer. A cash offer means that you have the funds readily available to purchase the co-op apartment without relying on a mortgage loan. While mortgage offers are common and widely accepted in the co-op market, they may not carry the same level of appeal as a cash offer. Sellers often prefer cash offers because they offer a greater level of certainty and reduce the risk of potential financing issues that could arise during the process. Ultimately, while the purchase price may not be subject to negotiation in most co-op transactions, presenting a cash offer can make your offer more attractive to the seller and increase your chances of securing the co-op apartment.

The seller may accept your offer as is, or they may counter with a different price or terms. Negotiations continue until both parties reach a mutual agreement on the purchase price and contract terms.

It's important to recognize that there are often other buyers who also consider it one of the best options within their budget range. In the co-op market, negotiations on the purchase price are typically limited compared to condos or homes. Co-ops usually have set prices determined by the board or the seller, leaving little room for negotiation.

However, there are other factors that can make your offer more appealing to the seller, such as the type of offer you present. One significant distinction is between a cash offer and a mortgage offer. A cash offer means that you have the funds readily available to purchase the co-op apartment without relying on a mortgage loan. While mortgage offers are common and widely accepted in the co-op market, they may not carry the same level of appeal as a cash offer. Sellers often prefer cash offers because they offer a greater level of certainty and reduce the risk of potential financing issues that could arise during the process. Ultimately, while the purchase price may not be subject to negotiation in most co-op transactions, presenting a cash offer can make your offer more attractive to the seller and increase your chances of securing the co-op apartment.

During my purchasing process, I encountered an interesting situation where the seller of the co-op unit also served as a board member of the building. While it is generally understood that a seller should not be involved in their own selling process, the seller's position as a board member provided unique insights into the board's decision-making criteria. With the assistance of my broker, we were able to directly communicate with the seller and address any questions or concerns regarding the board's evaluation criteria, specifically regarding the acceptance of different types of assets as post-closing liquid assets. Typically, liquid assets are those that can be easily converted to cash or cash equivalents. However, certain assets like retirement accounts may incur penalties if withdrawn early. Therefore, it is at the discretion of the board to determine which assets can be considered as post-closing liquid assets. By engaging with the seller, we were able to clarify these matters and obtain the necessary information without having to approach the board members separately.

3. ATTORNEY:

After you have submitted a pre-approved mortgage and personal financial statement in your offer, the seller's attorney will get back to you if the seller accepts your offer. Once your offer is accepted by a seller, a broker will request you to sign a non-disclosure agreement to proceed with the contract process.

At this time, it is essential to hire an attorney who will assist you in conducting due diligence and navigating the contract process.

The attorneys finalize the purchase agreement, and both the buyer and the seller sign the legally binding purchase contract. This document outlines the rights and obligations of each party, including the purchase price, deposit amount, closing date, and contingencies. Your attorney plays a crucial role in protecting your interests throughout the co-op purchase. They will review the co-op's financial statements, bylaws, offering plan, and minutes from board meetings to ensure there are no red flags or issues that may affect your decision to proceed. Additionally, they will conduct a thorough title search to identify any outstanding liens or encumbrances on the property. Throughout the process, your attorney will coordinate with the seller's attorney to facilitate a smooth transfer of funds and necessary documents.

In my purchasing experience, my broker introduced me to an attorney with a fixed fee of $2,000, 50% payable upon hiring and the remaining 50% due at the closing. It's important to discuss fees and payment terms with your attorney upfront to ensure clarity. Once you have hired your attorney, they will begin the due diligence on the target property. This involves reviewing all relevant documents related to the co-op building, conducting research, and addressing any potential issues that may arise going forward. Your attorney will guide you through each step, explaining the significance of the documents and advising you on any concerns they may uncover during their due diligence process.

I was fortunate to find a highly competent and helpful attorney. He was knowledgeable about the co-op purchase process and took the time to elaborate on each step. His patience and responsiveness made a significant difference in easing my anxieties during this nerve-wracking experience. As a first-time homebuyer, I understand that purchasing a home is a significant financial undertaking and can be quite overwhelming. Even after viewing multiple co-ops and finding what seemed to be the best fit, the process still carried a level of stress. Having an attorney who could provide reassurance and talk me through each step was invaluable.

4. CONTRACT:

Once the attorneys have finalized the purchase agreement, both the buyer and the seller proceed to sign the purchase contract. This pivotal document, which holds legal significance, outlines the rights and obligations of each party involved.

The signing process is typically facilitated using electronic signatures, such as DocuSign. This efficient method allows for the swift completion of the signing process, typically taking only a few minutes to complete, eliminating the need for physical paperwork, and reducing the time and effort involved in the process.

In my own process, I carefully read through the entire contract and then scheduled a call with my attorney to go over the crucial points. This step allowed me to ensure that I understood the contract correctly and benefited from my attorney's expertise. Taking the time to review the contract myself and seek guidance from my attorney gave me the confidence to proceed, knowing that I had fully comprehended and complied with the terms of the agreement.

Upon signing the purchase contract for the cooperative, you are usually expected to make a deposit called "earnest money" or "good faith deposit", typically half of your down payment, and that money goes to a buyer's attorney escrow account. Then, you give permission to your attorney to transfer the deposit to a seller's attorney's escrow account. This earnest money deposit serves as a crucial indicator of your commitment and seriousness as a buyer. By paying 10% at the contract stage, you demonstrate your willingness to proceed with the purchase and expedite the process. It is important to note that the deposit is held in an escrow account until the closing, providing assurance to both parties involved.

For the remainder of your down payment, you will have to make a payment at the closing. Typically, there is a time gap of approximately three months from the date of the contract to the closing. During this period, it is important to manage your financial strategy effectively. If you are planning to liquidate your stocks for the remaining portion of your down payment, you should monitor your investment closely to ensure that you have sufficient funds available to complete the payment when the closing date arrives.

Remember, the earnest money represents your willingness to invest in the cooperative and move forward with the purchase. By fulfilling this financial obligation promptly, you establish yourself as a serious buyer, enhancing your chances of successfully acquiring the desired cooperative unit. In other words, unless you make this payment, the seller does not regard you as a serious buyer and can still look for another buyer. After signing a purchase contract and paying half the deposit, you are now legally in a contract. We will explore the contract contingent upon the lender's commitment momentarily.

5. DUE DILIGENCE:

After signing the purchase contract, you will have a specified period, typically a few weeks, to complete due diligence on the property with your attorney. This may include obtaining financing, conducting inspections, and reviewing the co-op's financial documents. This stage allows the buyer to thoroughly examine the co-op building's documents, financials, and any other relevant information. Throughout the due diligence process, a buyer can also ensure the accuracy of the listed information on the website and whatever the broker verbally explained to you, for example about the co-op sublet policy, financial requirement, and maintenance fees.

During the due diligence process, it is essential to examine not only the current financial state of the co-op but also any potential future expenses that could impact residents. Through my due diligence process, I discovered that the co-op has planned a renovation project. This project would result in an increase in the monthly maintenance fees, and the shareholders/residents would be responsible for the distributed project amount based on their portion of the co-op share. This additional expense meant that a new monthly fee of $200 would be added to the listed monthly maintenance fee for a period of three years to cover the costs of the construction.

Navigating such potential costs and understanding their impact is where the expertise of an attorney becomes invaluable. It highlighted the importance of conducting a thorough due diligence process and seeking professional guidance to ensure there are no surprises or unexpected financial burdens down the line. My attorney guided me through the due diligence process, ensuring that I had a clear understanding of all the financial aspects and sublet policies associated with the co-op, including any projected construction or renovation expenses.

6. MORTGAGE APPLICATION:

After you sign a purchase agreement, you have to pick your mortgage lender after getting quotes from several potential lenders and select the one that offers the best rate. The timing of the mortgage application is crucial, especially in combination with the co-op contract and the attorney's due diligence process. Once the co-op contract is signed, and the attorney begins their due diligence, it is the ideal time to initiate the mortgage application. As we walked through the choice of mortgage types between fixed rate and adjustable-rate mortgage loan, you need to choose the one that fits your needs.

In my own experience, I inquired with three banks, Chase, Wells Fargo, and TD Bank, for a 30-year loan of both fixed rate and adjustable-rate loan (5, 7, and 10-years fixed options). As a result, TD Bank offered the best rate in a 30-years adjustable loan with a 7-years fixed rate. In my personal view on the trend of mortgage rates, it would be more likely to go down within a 7-years lock-in period, and I would then refinance this TD Bank mortgage. Now, let's review what comes in the actual mortgage application process.

1. **Mortgage application requirements:** When applying for a mortgage, you are usually required to provide the following documents, including a government-issued ID, employment history, and proof of income, tax returns, pay stubs, and bank statements. The lender requires this information to assess your financial stability and determine your eligibility for a mortgage loan. As my legal residency status in the U.S. was under a work visa, I was directed to physically visit a TD Bank branch office and show a passport that includes the visa stamp page for additional verification process on my residency status. At the bank's branch office, TD Bank completed another form of the mortgage application of "permanent/non-

permanent resident verification", and they uploaded it in the mortgage application portal. This process only took about 20 minutes.

2. **Appraisal:** A professional appraiser assesses the value of the co-op building. This appraisal process helps the lender determine the appropriate loan amount based on the property's worth. The appraiser considers factors such as the condition of the building, its amenities, comparable sales in the same area, and market conditions. The appraiser visits the co-op building and thoroughly examines its size, condition, location, and any distinctive features it may have. Recent renovations or upgrades are also considered.

The appraiser compiles a comprehensive report, which includes their observations and an estimated value of the apartment. In my own process, the appraisal report included several similar listings in the Upper East Side area, comparing factors such as square footage, apartment condition, unit structure, building condition, and recently sold values. While the appraisal provides confidence to the lender that the loan is backed by a property of sufficient value, it also protects the buyer from overpaying for the co-op and serves as a safeguard for the lender's investment.

3. **Underwriting:** Once you submit your mortgage application, the lender initiates the underwriting process. Underwriting is a comprehensive evaluation of your financial situation, the property you intend to purchase, and the loan amount you are applying for. An underwriter, who is a trained professional employed by the lender, carefully reviews your application and

supporting documents to assess your creditworthiness, ability to repay the loan, and the value of the property. They analyze various factors, including your credit history, debt-to-income ratio, employment stability, and the appraisal of the property. Based on their analysis, the underwriter determines whether to approve or deny your mortgage application.

4. **Contract contingent upon lender's commitment:** A crucial aspect of the co-op legal agreement is the inclusion of a contract contingent upon the lender's commitment. This clause states that the purchase contract is binding only if you obtain the lender's approval for the mortgage. It provides protection for both the buyer and the seller, ensuring that the purchase agreement is valid only when financing is secured. If the lender does not provide a commitment for the loan, the contract becomes void, allowing the buyer to withdraw from the transaction without any financial penalties, and any deposit already paid will be returned to the buyer from the seller's escrow account.

5. **Credit history:** Your credit history and credit score significantly influence the mortgage application process. Lenders use this information to evaluate your creditworthiness and assess the level of risk associated with lending to you. A higher credit score generally increases your chances of obtaining a favorable mortgage loan with more favorable terms. On the other hand, a lower credit score may result in higher interest rates or even loan denial. It's crucial to maintain a good credit standing by paying bills on time, minimizing debt, and avoiding excessive credit inquiries during the mortgage application process.

Understanding the mortgage application process, the significance of a contract contingent upon the lender's commitment, the appraisal of the co-op building, and the underwriting process will empower you to navigate the mortgage application process successfully. By preparing the necessary documentation and maintaining good credit, you can enhance your chances of obtaining a mortgage loan in your favor.

7. BOARD PACKAGE:

After signing the contract, the clock starts ticking for you to fulfill your obligations. You are typically given two to three months after signing a purchase contract to reach the closing date. Failing to meet this deadline risks the contract expiring and potentially losing your down payment deposit.

Upon signing a purchase contract, your broker will grant you access to a portal for the board package. This board package and the subsequent board review process are crucial steps in purchasing a co-op apartment, involving the submission of a comprehensive set of documents and information to the co-op board for their review.

The board package application form should be accessible within the board package portal. You will provide all personal information, including your name, current address, family, and work experience. This form requires disclosure of all relevant parties involved in the transaction, including the seller as a shareholder, your attorney, your broker, your guarantor, gift giver, and others as needed. Transparency regarding the transaction's participants helps the board assess the overall transaction and ensure compliance with co-op regulations.

Promptly uploading and signing all required documents is essential for a smooth and timely process. I highly recommend scheduling a kick-off call with your broker to discuss each requested document at the outset. As you upload each document, your broker will review it and may leave a comment if any information is incomplete, such as a missing signature. It's advisable to check the portal daily to respond to these review comments promptly and address all requests in a timely manner. The following documents are typically requested during the board package review process:

1. **Reference letter from your current landlord:** If you are currently renting, you will need a letter of reference from your present landlord or managing agent. This letter should attest to your character as a responsible tenant. If you are a homeowner, indicate this on the purchase application. You can request your property management to prepare a signed letter, which is usually provided by email within a few days.

2. **Letter from bank:** You need to provide a letter from your bank stating the type of accounts you have, for example, checking and savings accounts, along with their respective account numbers. This letter is necessary for the board team to obtain your credit reports. You can visit your bank and request an account summary with the date and signature. The bank can prepare this letter within 10 minutes at no cost.

3. **Letter from employer:** You need to submit a letter from your employer stating your job function, length of employment, and annual compensation. If you are self-employed, not employed, or retired, a letter from a certified public accountant verifying your income is

required. Usually, letters from third-party employment verification services are not accepted. If you receive a bonus, you should request your employer to include the bonus from the previous year and the current year to show the consistency of your salary. The letter must be on your company's letterhead and signed.

4. **Personal and professional reference letters:** You have to include two personal reference letters from individuals who know you well and can vouch for your qualifications as a cooperative community member. Additionally, you need to include two professional reference letters from colleagues or business associates who can attest to your professional character. I would suggest that you explain the tone and nuance of the reference letter contents to your reference letter writers so that they can recommend you as a great addition to a co-op community. The letter can be in any format, but it must be signed and dated.

5. **Federal tax return:** You must provide your federal tax returns for the past two years to demonstrate a comprehensive overview of your personal finances. This can also prove the consistency of your income over two years. If you are paid on a commission basis or any other means that are not consistent, it can make it difficult to support that you won't have any difficulties with recurring maintenance and mortgage payments. You should provide additional support to show the co-op board that you will not have any issues with monthly maintenance fees and mortgage payments.

6. **Appraisal report:** You need to upload an appraisal report provided by your mortgage lender that validates

the value of the co-op apartment. Your lender performs an appraisal on your co-op unit to process the mortgage application, and they should be able to provide you with an appraisal report at this stage. You just need to receive it from your lender and upload it to the board package portal.

7. **Personal financial statement:** You need to prepare a personal financial statement in a format provided within the board package portal that summarizes all of your assets, debts, gross income, and any other financial items. Each piece of this financial statement summary has to be substantiated by providing official supporting documents such as bank statements, investment account statements, 401(k) statements, retirement account statements, debt statements, and more. As each document probably has a different statement date, for example by month or quarter, you just need to upload the latest available document to the portal. If you received a gift, for example from parents, that is going to be applied for your co-op down payment, you need to upload a gift letter that is notarized and signed by the gift giver.

8. **Cover letter:** You should start drafting a cover letter in one to two pages addressed to the co-op board team, introducing yourself, describing your financial condition, explaining why you are attracted to the property, and assuring the board of your commitment to being a respectful resident in the co-op community. I recommend that you start with what brought you to New York City and how you like the city. You should also include your work responsibility, personal finance responsibility, your hobbies, and your personality, ensuring that these can fit the co-op community. You should make sure that this

cover letter summarizes all information submitted to the board portal and demonstrates that you are a great candidate.

9. **Mortgage application and commitment letter:** You are most likely required to include the completed mortgage loan application and commitment letter provided by your lender. A mortgage commitment letter confirms your eligibility for a loan, yet it is not full approval. Mortgage commitment letters ensure a seller and buyer that a loan application aligns with the lender's requirements and the likelihood of having their offers accepted, and aids in budgeting for homes within their price range.

10. **Aztec agreement:** You will need to submit an Aztec agreement. An Aztec agreement establishes an acknowledgment between you, your lender, and the co-op corporation management that the lender will have a first lien on the buyer's shares and proprietary lease as collateral for the loan. It is required for purchasing a co-op apartment with financing. During my purchasing process, my attorney prepared the Aztec agreement and mailed three sets of original documents to me. These identical documents are going to be signed by a buyer, lender, and co-op management at the end of the application process. A buyer uploads an electronic version of the Aztec documents to a portal and mails the originals to a co-op management.

11. **Others:** There are several additional documents that are already provided within the board package portal, and you just need to read and sign them. These documents include a lead paint disclosure, house rules, fire safety guidelines, credit view consent form, apartment

alteration form, tax abatement form, proposed purchasers' acknowledgment, bed bug disclosure form, and more. You should read all these documents thoroughly and make sure that you understand them to avoid any potential issues going forward.

It is worth reviewing the cost of the board application. You will pay the board package fee through the board package application portal. The breakdown of costs may include an application fee of $950, a credit check fee of $250, and a corporation administrative fee of $25. Throughout the purchase process, you may encounter one-time fees that are not cheap, so it is always recommended to set aside a financial buffer for miscellaneous fees.

Once all the required documents are signed and submitted, a broker will review the entire board package before forwarding it to the co-op board for assessment. The board will then schedule an interview to further evaluate your candidacy as a potential co-op owner.

8: BOARD INTERVIEW:

The board assessment process begins after you have submitted all the required documents into the board portal and completed the application. This assessment involves various parties, including the co-op board, brokers, sellers, lenders, and co-op management, all working together to evaluate your eligibility and ensure a smooth transition into the co-op community. These board members are all residents of the building.

Once your application is submitted, the co-op board reviews your financial and personal background. They carefully assess your financial stability, creditworthiness, and ability to meet co-op financial obligations. If they find your application promising, they will invite you for an interview, which is typically conducted by board members. The interview allows the board members to get to know you better and gauge your compatibility with the co-op community.

It is important to keep in your mind that this is not a job interview, and the goal is not to sell yourself or impress the interviewers. Instead, focus on providing concise and clear answers to their questions while maintaining a friendly and approachable demeanor.

My interview was via a video call with the four interviewers, and it took around 30 minutes. As the co-op board participants are solely volunteering their time, the interview dates were only on weekdays. I would recommend dressing in business casual attire. During the interview, the board members will inquire about your background, lifestyle, and why you like this building. To enhance your chances of success, consider the following tips and share unique stories that can leave a lasting impression.

Community contribution: You should understand the co-op culture, rules, and values to tailor your answers and demonstrate your alignment. They want to see your community ethics. I suggest showcasing your contributions and share a story about a community initiative you spearheaded or a project where you collaborated with others to make a positive impact. This presents your commitment to community engagement.

- During my interview, I shared a story that I volunteered for a New York based Japanese soccer community through supporting a marketing and blog team. I oversaw the team's blog update that help the team to share its presence and activities, which would attract new players to join the team and team sponsors. This team is not only a soccer team, but also a community that provides an opportunity for Japanese and whoever interested in Japanese cultures to find a New York based Japanese community. I happily volunteered to be part of the operation team as an immigrant to America from Japan.

Highlight your personal finance: Be ready to share the highlight of your personal financial statement that you submitted in the board package. If asked, share a personal anecdote about how you manage your personal finances wisely and your spending priority. This demonstrates resilience and responsible financial management. For example, you are paying off your student loans while achieving your monthly saving and investing plan. You can also share your career plan to demonstrate your vision with your personal finance and responsibilities.

- During my interview, the boards members inquired about my career path in the next several years whether if I go for promotion or seek for different career path. It can give the board an idea of my personality and personal finance and assessing potential changes in my income structures such as a fixed salary, commission base, self-employee and as such. It can also indicate any possibility of your relocation along with your career progression.

Be engaged: The board team would like to get to know you aside from the board package documents. You want to present yourself genuine, enthusiastic, and approachable and make your response in a concise and clear fashion. During my interview, the board members asked what I like to do in my free time, favorites musicians, and what I like about New York city. You should show a genuine interest in the co-op community and neighborhood.

- I would recommend you share one memorable experience that shaped your values to be part of a close-knit community. I shared a story from my graduate school program where I volunteered to be a teaching assistant for Japanese class to be engaged with students and school. Throughout this teaching assistant experience, I enjoyed going through their learning journey and being able to assist their progress. These stories would give the board team a good picture of you being a part of the community-based residence.

It is always recommended to send a thank-you email after your interview to appreciate their time and an opportunity to get to know the board members. Usually after a few days or even on the same day of interview, the board will let you know if you are accepted and approved. At this stage, you are done with most of your parts in a co-op purchase process. You will proceed to the closing processes that include the final assessment of the property, purchase contract closing, and move-in scheduling. Your broker, seller, lender, and co-op management will continue to assist you throughout these stages.

9. CLOSING:

Regarding the final assessment of the property, you, your representative broker, and possibly a representative from the co-op board will perform a walk-through of the apartment for a final viewing to ensure there are no new damages or issues before your move-in. Following the final assessment, the closing process begins. During the closing process, you will make the payment of the remaining portion of the down payment. This means that if you had already paid half of the deposit upon signing the contract, you need to pay the remaining half at the closing.

Your attorney will also work with the co-op management to fulfill any additional requirements or paperwork necessary for the purchase. Additionally, your attorney will set a closing date scheduling with all participants for a closing meeting, including the buyer, buyer's attorney, buyer's broker, seller, seller's broker, seller's attorney, mortgage lender, and co-op management.

On the closing day, a stock certificate for the cooperative apartment along with other documentation is handed to the buyer, and the total purchase price is given to the seller. This closing meeting usually takes place at the cooperative's managing agent's office on weekdays and typically lasts around two hours.

Additionally, in case the seller has a mortgage, a seller's lender will collect a mortgage payoff check and drop off the original stock certificate at the closing. If you take a mortgage for your purchasing, your representative lender takes an ownership of the original stock certificate and proprietary lease at the closing until you pay off your mortgage. When you are under contract to sell your apartment on the other hand, your attorney will need to contact your bank before the anticipated closing date to arrange to have your bank deliver the original documents to the closing. Often banks take several weeks or more to locate and send these documents to their attorneys. The bank's attorneys will then send a representative to the closing to deliver the stock certificate and lease upon receipt of a check paying off your loan.

In case you cannot physically attend a closing meeting due to traveling or any other responsibilities, your attorney can prepare a power of attorney document that allows your attorney to act certain legal procedures on behalf of you and sign all paperwork for you at the closing. In my own closing, I had to request the power of attorney as I already had a planned international travel on the closing day. The overall co-op purchase is a long process involving multiple parties and it is not easy to predict the closing timeline. When it comes to setting a closing meeting date, if you request closing date at a further date or try to reschedule the closing date, it might incur additional fees for moving other parties' schedules and it creates additional paperwork on your latest financial documents.

After the closing, the co-op management will provide you with a move-in schedule. This schedule outlines the logistics and guidelines for moving into the co-op. It includes details such as move-in dates, elevator reservations, and any other necessary arrangements to ensure a smooth transition into your new home. Throughout the entire process, your broker serves as your guide, providing expert advice, facilitating communication, and assisting with negotiations and paperwork.

As you settle into your new home, take the time to familiarize yourself with the building's rules and regulations. Get to know your neighbors and actively participate in the coop community. Embrace the benefits of coop living, such as shared amenities and collective decision-making, as you enjoy the advantages of owning real estate in the vibrant city of New York. In the next and final chapter, we will briefly touch on some points that I suggest keeping in your mind after you move in your new apartment.

CHAPTER 7

Post-purchase

There are several aspects related to financial wealth and future revaluation of costs and lifestyle that you want to keep in mind. These considerations can help you make informed decisions and avoid potential troubles. Let us briefly review these points.

1. **Shareholder meeting:** It would be a good idea to attend shareholder meetings and contribute ideas to enhance community engagement. You can also stay informed about any updates on co-op policies from these meetings. There may even be opportunities to become a board member after residing for several years.

Typically, the board consists of four officers: president, vice president, secretary, and treasurer. They respond to changes in the physical and financial status of the building, economic environment, maintenance fees, and other co-op operational decisions. If you possess knowledge in areas such as real estate, legal matters, finance, or accounting, your expertise would be a valuable addition to the board.

2. **Refinancing:** If you financed your apartment purchase, regularly consider refinancing options to lower the interest expense on your mortgage. Refinancing involves reviewing your mortgage plan, potentially changing from fixed-rate to adjustable-rate loans, adjusting the loan

term, or securing a better interest rate. Opting for a 15-year loan can substantially reduce the amount of interest paid over the mortgage's life. If mortgage rates reach historic lows, consider locking in the rate with a 30-year fixed-rate loan, as potential gains from other investments could outweigh mortgage expenses.

3. **Maintenance fee:** Budget your monthly mortgage payment at a fixed amount unless stated otherwise in your mortgage agreement. However, your monthly maintenance fees are subject to increase based on inflation adjustments. While these increases may not be significant, they should be factored into your financial planning. Additionally, pay attention to potential capital expenditures, as the costs may be allocated to co-op shareholders based on their shares. Actively staying informed about upgrades and participating in the decision-making process can help you prepare your budget accordingly.

4. **Capital gain relief:** When you sell your primary residence, there is a capital gains tax exclusion benefit allowing you to exclude up to $250,000 in capital gains (or $500,000 if married and filing jointly) under IRS section 121 (IRS, Sale of your home, 2024). To qualify, you must have lived in the primary home for at least two out of the past five years. Understanding this capital gain relief can help you plan for future moves.

5. **Renovation:** Before remodeling your apartment, familiarize yourself with the co-op's renovation guidelines, obtain necessary approvals, and communicate effectively with the co-op board. Failure to do so may result in penalties and legal complications.

6. **Other tax benefits:** Besides your primary residential home, if you're interested in purchasing an investment property, there are several tax benefits worth noting:

When selling an investment property, you can defer capital gains if you reinvest the proceeds into another like-kind investment property within 180 days. If you follow this rule, you can defer your capital gain indefinitely (IRS, Like-Kind Exchanges, 2024).

You should also be aware of tax-deductible items as you rent an investment property and generate rental income. Mortgage interest and depreciation expenses on your investment property are tax-deductible, offsetting gross rental income and lowering taxable income. Other operating expenses for rental operations, such as repairs, maintenance, insurance, and property taxes, are also tax-deductible.

Closure

As we conclude our journey through the process of purchasing a co-op apartment, it's essential to reflect on the experience and acknowledge the significance of closure. I trust that this book has guided you through a comprehensive journey, unraveling the intricacies of purchasing a co-op apartment in New York City. Across various chapters, we've delved into crucial steps, considerations, and financial aspects integral to this process. However, it's paramount to recognize that cooperative ownership transcends mere financial implications; it must harmonize with your career trajectory, life aspirations, and personal affinity for the city.

With the real estate market and interest rates in a constant state of flux, staying abreast of market trends and fluctuations is imperative. Moreover, comprehending the interplay between rental expenses and apartment ownership costs empowers you to make informed housing decisions. Each cooperative has unique set of rules and regulations, necessitating a thorough exploration of your chosen co-op building's provisions, such as subleasing options, to ensure alignment with your long-term objectives.

I must stress that the insights and perspectives shared in this book draw from my personal experiences and knowledge up to the time of writing. It's prudent to remain updated with the latest information, seek advice from professionals, and conduct meticulous research before making significant decisions.

Closure

Before closing this book, I want to emphasize three points in short. Firstly, it's entirely normal to experience overwhelming feelings of anxiety when purchasing your first home, given its significant financial commitment. As a financially responsible individual, transitioning to homeownership represents a new level of accountability, which may evoke hesitancy in utilizing your savings.

Secondly, as the purchase journey progresses from browsing listings to securing a mortgage, it's natural to question the validity of your decision repeatedly. Transitioning from a casual observer to a committed buyer is a significant leap, inevitably accompanied by bouts of nervousness. However, dedicating ample time to review personal finances, conduct thorough research, and simulate your purchase can bolster your confidence in the decision-making process.

Lastly, purchasing your first home offers a profound opportunity for self-discovery. Beyond financial planning, it prompts reflection on non-financial facets that shape your life. Considerations such as career aspirations, preferred lifestyle, city preferences, family dynamics, and apartment criteria play pivotal roles in aligning your financial journey with your broader life goals. While Excel spreadsheets may aid in numerical simulations, they often fall short in capturing life's uncertainties. Nonetheless, by incorporating conservative assumptions, you can navigate toward informed decisions that resonate with your unique circumstances. This transformative process not only shapes your financial trajectory but also unveils insights into your values and priorities.

About the Author

Kento, hailing from Kyoto, Japan, spent 27 formative years in his hometown before embarking on a new chapter in Los Angeles for graduate school. With a robust background in finance and accounting, Kento is a Certified Public Accountant (CPA) boasting over 9 years of experience in financial auditing and due diligence, both in Japan and the United States. This book marks his debut as an author, and he is already contemplating his next literary venture.

Works Cited

Bankrate. (2024). *How The Fed's Rate Decisions Move Mortgage Rates*. Retrieved from Bankrate: https://www.bankrate.com/mortgages/federal-reserve-and-mortgage-rates/#:~:text=Factors%20that%20influence%20mortgage%20rates&text=Typically%2C%20the%20gap%2

Brookings. (2023). *Mortgage rate and US Treasury Bond*. Retrieved from Brookings: https://www.brookings.edu/articles/high-mortgage-rates-are-probably-here-for-a-while/

Cooperatornews. (2023). *From the Gilded Age to the Present - A History of Cooperative Housing in NYC*. Retrieved from Cooperatornews: https://cooperatornews.com/article/a-history-of-cooperative-housing-in-nyc

D., G. (n.d.). *NYC Condo history*. Retrieved from Cooperatornews: https://cooperatornews.com/article/a-history-of-cooperative-housing-in-nyc

Hauseit. (2024). *Buyer Closing Cost Calculator*. Retrieved from Hauseit: https://www.hauseit.com/closing-cost-calculator-for-buyer-nyc/#:~:text=Buying%20a%20coop%20in%20NYC%20takes%20around%203%20months%20from

HUD. (2024). *Loans*. Retrieved from U.S. Department of Housing and Urban Development: https://www.hud.gov/buying/loans

IRS. (2024). *Capital gain exclusion.* Retrieved from Internal Revenue Service: www.irs.gov. Published March 17, 2024. https://www.irs.gov/taxtopics/tc701

IRS. (2024). *Like-Kind Exchanges.* Retrieved from Internal Revenue Service: www.irs.gov. https://www.irs.gov/businesses/small-businesses-self-employed/like-kind-exchanges-real-estate-tax-tips

IRS. (2024). *Mortgage Interest.* Retrieved from Internal Revenue Service: https://www.irs.gov/faqs/itemized-deductions-standard-deduction/real-estate-taxes-mortgage-interest-points-other-property-expenses/real-estate-taxes-mortgage-interest-points-other-property-expenses-5#:~:text=If%20the%20home%20was%20acquired%20after%20Dece

IRS. (2024). *Property tax deduction limit.* Retrieved from Internal Revenue Service: https://www.irs.gov/taxtopics/tc503#:~:text=Overall%20limit

IRS. (2024). *Sale of your home.* Retrieved from Internal Revenue Service: https://www.irs.gov/taxtopics/tc701

IRS. (2024). *Standard deduction.* Retrieved from Internal Revenue Service: https://www.irs.gov/publications/p505#:~:text=For%202024%2C%20the%20standard%20deduction,Head%20of%20Household%E2%80%94%2421%2C900.

Midland States Bank. (2024). *FHA, VA, and USDA Home Mortgage Loans.* Retrieved from Midland States Bank: https://www.midlandsb.com/mortgage/fha-va-usda-loans#:~:text=VA%20and%20USDA%20loans%20offer

NYC 311. (2024). *Rent Increases*. Retrieved from NYC 311:
https://portal.311.nyc.gov/article/?kanumber=KA-03296

Prevu. (2024). *Seller Closing Cost*. Retrieved from Prevu:
https://www.prevu.com/blog/seller-closing-costs-nyc

Realty Collective. (2022). *Property tax within coop maintenance fees*. Retrieved from Realty Collective:
https://realtycollective.com/what-coop-costs-are-tax-deductible/#:~:text=A%20Portion%20of%20Maintenance%20Fees%3A&text=Th

Renthop. (2024). *Renthop*. Retrieved from Average Rent in NYC:
https://www.renthop.com/average-rent-in/upper-east-side-new-york-ny

Smartasset. (2024). *New York Paycheck/Tax Rate Calculator*. Retrieved from SmartAsset. :
https://smartasset.com/taxes/new-york-paycheck-calculator

Stevens, B. H. (2022). *NYC Coop history*. Retrieved from Brown Harris Stevens: https://www.blog.bhsusa.com/post/3-numbers-to-know-before-purchasing-an-nyc-co-op#:~:text=Buyers%20will%20typically%20need%20a

The Mortgage Reports. (2023). *Conventional loan limits for 2024*. Retrieved from The Mortgage Reports:
https://themortgagereports.com/27773/2017-conforming-mortgage-loan-limits-fannie-mae-freddie-ma

Made in the USA
Las Vegas, NV
04 December 2024

13408885R00046